# THE MISEDUCATION OF
# CREDIT

# DREA DIANE

# THE MISEDUCATION OF CREDIT

## Copyright © 2023 Drea Diane

Library of Congress Control Number: 2023907993

# Table of Contents

# Foreword

I remember the first time I met Drea. We were in training together and realized we had the same phone, a Sidekick. We often joke that one of us said, "Do you want to be my friend?" I'm sure it was her. That was the introduction of a friendship that would shape a huge part of my adult life. I soon learned that, like myself, she was studying for her MBA. We started going to the bookstore to study. Well, I was studying, and Drea was walking around. As we navigated through life, our friendship was always consistent. I got married, had two children, started jobs, left jobs, filed for bankruptcy, started several businesses, became successful, and much more, and guess what? She was there.

As someone who has become an advocate for financial freedom and money management, I was so excited when she started writing her book. I've witnessed her train in every capacity, from FB Live to a small conference room with teenagers, to a corporate environment. I've seen people come up to her in tears about how her information helped their credit scores increase by 200+ points. The thing that always stands out is that she did it differently. She gave the tools, but it was up to them to do the WORK. Do you know how it feels when you have to work to save up for a new pair of shoes? When you get them, it feels so much better because YOU earned them. YOU did it. A level of pride is instilled in you once you complete a course with 'The Financial Lifeline.'

The day she asked me to read *The Miseducation of Credit,* I asked, "Are you sure you want me to read it?" As someone with my own book club and who has read thousands of books in my lifetime, I'm not easy to impress as a reader. However, as I turned each page, I was eager to know what was next. She shares her financial experiences that might make you laugh or break your heart. It's honest, real, funny, and, most importantly, easy to understand. I've read finance books written above my pay grade and don't get past the third page. You feel me. I know you do. As you turn the pages to read this book, take your time. Really hear what she's saying and implement the things you need to change your financial outlook.

Drea, I'm incredibly excited for you! You walk through your life with grace, empathy, love, and light. I know that your father is extremely proud. It's been an honor to call you my best friend and sister. I pray that God blesses you in a way you'll never understand because of your obedience.

SAME GRACE,

Alysia Leyva

# Introduction

For years, I always wanted to be an asset to the world of financial literacy. I recognized that there is a huge lack and disconnect in the education field of understanding the importance and aspects of credit and budgeting. *The Miseducation of Credit* is a resource to help you heal financially. Discussing credit and finances can sometimes be intimidating. I want you to know that the modules in this book are thorough but easy to understand and follow. Understanding and learning how to read a credit report is one of the most important tools to creating a healthier financial life. I pray that this book gives you a boost in your confidence, financial peace, and helps increase your credit score.I also hope it teaches you how to manage your finances. This book was written to become a household name and to break financial generational curses. It's time to take control of your finances. You deserve to be financially healed!

Perseverance + Purpose = Progress

Class is in session

# Module 1

## Not the typical dinner conversation

Growing up in the early 80s, this was the era both parents worked in my family. Understanding credit wasn't the topic of discussion at dinner. As a matter of fact, it wasn't discussed in school either. It wasn't until my first year in college that I purchased my first car. I can remember this day as if it was yesterday. I walked into the Hyundai dealership and picked out the car I wanted. It was the brand new all-white Hyundai Sonata, with the leather interior, beautiful dashboard, and baaabbyyy, I was ready to put some tint on my windows. Then boom, my feelings were immediately hurt. I was crushed, and the excitement immediately left my body. I remember the salesman mentioning that I needed a co-signer and a down payment. My mind went into a fog, and a look of confusion rested on my face. It was obvious that I didn't know what a "co-signer" was, nor did I understand how a down payment works and what that meant. I called a few people and asked them to co-sign for me for a brand-new car. I was told, "No," "My credit isn't good enough," and a few even laughed. I now understand why they laughed. I was asking them to take on a huge responsibility and possibly take on a burden in the event I couldn't afford to make my car payments. I now laugh at my audacity to get mad when I got those responses.

Despite it all, there was a teachable lesson in receiving the "No" responses. At that moment, I began to study and learn the world of credit for myself. I made myself familiar with the most used terminology. As I got older, my hunger for learning this industry progressed. I loved it so much that I dedicated 23 years of my life to this industry. My passion progressed, and I decided to become certified as an Accredited Financial Coach. I worked 17 years in the credit union industry and was placed in one of the most awkward positions. As a part of my job, I had to not only approve loans but decline them as well. The hard part was when I had to inform the member that their loan was declined. In most cases, I empathized with the customers. But there was nothing in my will that I could do as it related to coaching them on how to protect and work on their credit that would have allowed them to, in the near future, place themselves in a better financial position with their credit health and score.

As you read this book and break down the modules, I challenge you to incorporate these tools to become a part of the daily or weekly discussion at the dinner table. I know family dinner isn't much of the norm anymore, so create or incorporate this into the family group text or virtual meetings. Challenge each other to understand credit and savings, prioritize needs vs. wants, and become familiar with the terminology in the glossary at the end of this book. I encourage you to break generational curses. The saying "knowledge is power" is true. You can be stripped of all material things, but there's one thing you can always stand on: your intellect. Let's change the trajectory of a lack of knowledge or fear when it comes to financial literacy. As you begin to read this book and study, I pray that God gives you the wisdom, patience, understanding, and willingness to take control of your financial situation. Grab your pen, paper, and highlighter, and MANIFEST what you want!

You got this!

# Module 2

## What is Credit?

Credit is your financial power. It is an agreement where the borrower (you) and the lender or merchant agrees to give you funding based on your ability to pay it back. Borrowing funds are contractual and finalized by an oral, verbal, or documented contract. Your borrowing power is developed on a relationship of TRUST. Here, money is given to you on the contractual agreement, and the lender or merchant trusts you will pay them back. Not only pay them back but also on time and, most times, with interest.

The history of credit was very intriguing as I was doing my research. Let's dig into it. Credit was established in the 1800s and was only available to business owners then. Before the 1960s, there were over 2000 credit bureaus. Over the last 20 years, we now have three major credit bureaus: TransUnion, Equifax, and Experian. The three credit bureaus used the FICO and Vantage scores to create a scoring factor. The FICO score is the most commonly used matrix, and there are 16 versions of FICO. The FICO score comprises 5 factors: payment history, debt utilization, length of credit history, mixed credit, and new accounts. The components of these scoring factors can break or make you. Here's what you need to know about the two.

# Module 3

## FICO vs. Vantage Score

### Why is my score different on all three credit reports?

In most cases, you will sometimes have three different scores on each credit report. The reason is that many creditors do not report your account history to all three credit bureaus. When applying for credit for a particular merchant, be sure to get clarification that they will report your account history to TransUnion, Equifax, and Experian.

Two types of scoring factors will make up your credit score. There is the Vantage score and FICO Score. Let's break down the two.

### Vantage score:

The Vantage score, in some aspects, is similar to FICO as it relates to the scoring range. Conversely, the Vantage score weighs four components of your credit based on its influence. The four components are amounts owed (utilization, balances, and available credit), payment history, depth of credit, and recent credit applications. The Vantage score allows you a 14-day window to car shop and shop for your mortgage lender. In contrast, FICO allows you 45 days to shop without having a possible negative impact on your credit score. The Vantage score is most commonly used by lenders for auto loans, credit cards, banking, and personal and Fintech loans.

## FICO Score:

FICO (Fair Isaac Corporation) is a scoring factor comprising data collected from credit bureaus. There are different models of FICO. "FICO also has different variations of its basic scoring model tailored to different types of lenders (for example, home loans or car loans). So, you could have several different FICO scores, even when they are all calculated from the same credit agency's data."
(https://www.consumerfinance.gov/ask-cfpb/what-is-a-fico-score-en-1883/#:~:text=FICO%20stands%20for%20the%20Fair,collected%20by%20credit%20reporting%20agencies.).

The FICO credit score ranges from 300-850. There are five components to the FICO score: Payment History, Debt Utilization, Length of credit history, Mixture of credit, and new credit. In the next section of this book, we will discuss the weight of each component and how to master carrying the weight of them all.

Here is a more detailed point breakdown of the scoring factors.

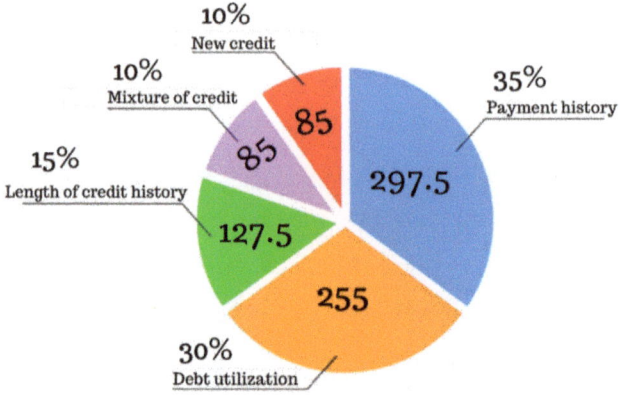

10%
New credit

10%
Mixture of credit

85

85

15%
Length of credit history

127.5

35%
Payment history

297.5

255

30%
Debt utilization

FICO credit score point basis

## Vantage Score

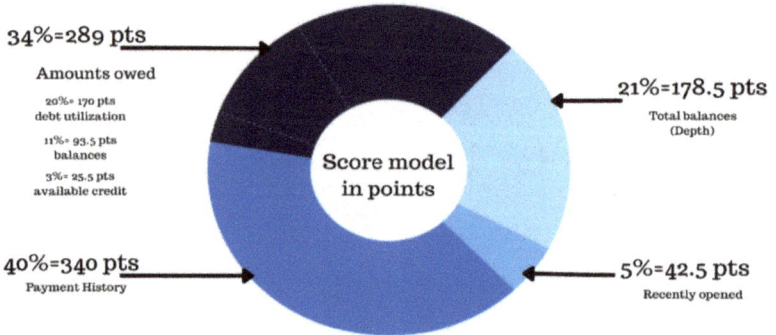

34%=289 pts

Amounts owed

20%= 170 pts
debt utilization

11%= 93.5 pts
balances

3%= 25.5 pts
available credit

21%=178.5 pts

Total balances
(Depth)

Score model
in points

40%=340 pts

Payment History

5%=42.5 pts

Recently opened

# Module 4

## The 5 components of credit and its impact.

## Payment history 35%

### FICO:

Your payment history makes up 35% of your FICO credit score; that is more than 1/3 of your score. 35% of 850 is almost 298 points. That is HUGE! This means you must be disciplined in making on-time payments on all open accounts. For example, suppose you neglect missing payments on all accounts past the 30-day reporting grace period. In that case, your credit score can now become 552! Now, of course, many times, this isn't the case. Missing one, yes, just one payment can decrease your credit score by up to 150 points.

If you aren't disciplined enough, set your payments on "Auto Pay." Autopay guarantees your payment will be timely and stress-free of negative credit reporting.

### Vantage:

As you have read, your Vantage score comprises four components. In this scoring model, your Payment history is extremely influential (40%),

Credit Utilization is highly influential (34%), Total balances and debt are moderately influential (21%), and recently opened accounts and the total amount of debt are less influential (5%).

A missed payment is extremely influential on the Vantage scoring model and consists of 40% of your score. 40% of your score is approximately 340 points! One, two, or three missed payments or repeated behavior of negligent payments can cost you your credit score to become as low as 510.

Why did I say "cost?" I used the word "cost" because your credit score determines your interest rate, payment amount, and loan conditions with stipulations from the underwriters and lenders. A lower credit score can cost you thousands of dollars in interest, which will further "cost" you to overpay 2 to 3 times over the original price.

## Debt Utilization 30%:

This is where the fun begins!! This is the part that credit card lenders won't teach you. Of course not; they are in business to make money. When you are issued a credit card, I want you to think of it as a revolving door. Except, this time, when you go through the revolving door (after reading this book), I want you to not allow your credit card debt to follow behind you. You may ask, "What do you mean, Drea?" I'm glad you asked. Often, you may notice that you're making on-time payments, but your credit score is stagnant or decreasing. That is because your debt utilization is too high. You can start by using the 30% rule and apply the 20% or 10% rule depending on your financial budget. These rules can be applied by this calculation: multiply your card limit by 30%, i.e., if your limit is $1000.00, you will multiply $1000.00 x 30%, which equals $300.00. This means that each month when your credit card statement closes, your balance should be $300 or less. That is what will be reported to the credit bureaus each month. Let's do another calculation using the 20% rule. If your credit limit is $2,650.00, you will multiply $2,650 x 20%, which equals $530.00. Below, I want you to calculate your credit utilization using the 30% rule (use a pencil).

_____ X _____ = _____

_____ X _____ = _____

_____ X _____ = _____

_____ X _____ = _____

_____ X _____ = _____

## Length of credit history 15%

When looking at what makes up your credit score, your length of credit history makes up 15% of your score. Keep in mind that the longer your account is open and in good standing, the greater your credit length impacts your score. Opening new accounts can/will affect your length of credit history. To determine your age of credit, you will add your oldest and newest accounts in months and then divide them by the number of accounts in total.

For example:

Accounts on a credit report

- ABC Credit= 12 years (144 months)

- Auto Lending Finance 7 years (56 months)

- South Mortgage Co. = 15 years (180 months)

Let's determine the length of credit history. We will add up 144 + 56 + 180 = 380 months. You will now divide 380 (months in total)/ 3 (total accounts/tradelines) = 126 months, which is equivalent to 10.5 years in the age of credit history. As you can see, your oldest account is 15 years old, but once you begin to open new accounts, it reduces the credit age. With this only weighing 15% of the impact on your credit, it is critical to lenders as they will determine your creditworthiness. Lenders and underwriters are looking to see how long you have had this account and how well you took care of your account with previous lenders. They analyze your relationship with other lenders to see if they can trust you. While applying for credit, be sure it benefits you as the consumer. This next section will discuss the importance of when and when not to apply for "new credit."

## New Credit 10%

Growing up, I thought that having a million credit cards was the way of life and that I would be featured on the "Rich & Famous" LOL! Not at all; I was ignorant of this in my 20s while shopping in the stores. I had department store credit cards that didn't fit my needs AT ALL. I absolutely WANTED the credit cards but didn't NEED them. I had credit cards to Toys R Us and Children's place... Why? I didn't have kids! I should have just applied for a Pet Smart card while at it. All jokes aside, be sure to apply for credit cards with low-interest rates while applying for credit cards. I recommend applying at your bank or credit union, where you have built rapport. The average interest rate for a department store credit card is 24.99% (wow). Yes, I know it sounds great when they say, "you can save 10% today on your purchase if approved.". If I'm being honest, you are only saving on the taxes you will pay for that purchase. I want you to think about your interest rate vs. a 10% one-time savings and the long-term accrued interest and finance charges if you drag out your payment by paying the minimum monthly payment. In the beginning, the approval gives you peace and confidence and seems affordable. I want you to pay attention to your credit card statements and review how long it will take to pay off your balance with the minimum payment and how much interest/finance charges you will accrue over time.

When applying for new credit, remember you have incurred a new "inquiry" to be reported to the credit bureaus. Inquiries will remain on your credit report for 2 years. Can they impact your credit score? In some instances, yes, they can. If you are applying for credit at random times, it can decrease your credit score. If you are shopping for a new car or the best mortgage loan, you are given a 14–45-day window to avoid having a heavy negative impact on your score. Be intentional when applying for credit.

There are two types of inquiries: soft inquires and hard inquiries. A soft inquiry is when a company or person has limited access to your credit report for screening or promotional offers. They are typically used for "pre-approval" on credit card offers and employment verification. A soft inquiry will show on your credit report but will only be visible to you and not affect your credit score. A hard inquiry is visible to you and any other lenders when you apply for new credit with your permission. Having multiple hard inquiries when applying for credit can affect your credit score when applying randomly and often. If you are applying for a mortgage, I would advise that you shop for your loans within a 14-day window. If you notice on your credit report that there are inquiries you didn't authorize, contact the lender. If that doesn't work, dispute the inaccurate reporting through the credit reporting agencies.

## Mixed Credit 10%

A diversified credit report is a plus in the world of credit. Creditors, lenders, and underwriters would like to see your behavior pattern with different types of accounts on your credit report. Having a mixture of credit consists of having tradelines/accounts that consist of a mortgage, installment (vehicle loan, personal loan), revolving (credit card, HELOC), and student loans.

While conducting a coaching session, I am often asked, "What should I do with my "charge-off account?" "Should I pay it off or leave it on my credit report?". In all honesty, the answer to this question truly depends on your financial goals. I mean, if you are considering purchasing a home or securing some type of loan, the lender/underwriter may question that particular account and require that the debt is satisfied before they approve your loan application. A lender may also attach stipulations (require a down payment, shorter loan term, and approve less than what's requested) to the loan approval in the event the debt is minimal or their approval guidelines aren't strict. I also will encourage you to check the statute of limitation in your state to see when your debt may fall off or if the creditor is no longer legally allowed to sue. I want you to keep in mind that if you make any contact with the creditor, make a payment, or conduct any activity on that account, you have now started your date of delinquency over. For example, if you have an account charged off for six years as of Jan. 1, 2022, and decide to satisfy the debt and have contacted the creditor to make a payment on Mar. 1, 2022, your new date of activity will be that date of your last transaction. And you now have a "new" charge-off account. Your activity will restart the charge-off date. The creditor now has seven years instead of one more year (depending on your state) to seek payment and/or take legal action.

I want you to identify why the account became delinquent and, just like any account, validate if you are legally liable for the debt. Yes, you may have opened the account, but remember that the FCRA law protects you from inaccurate reporting *winks eye*.

**\*Disclaimer:** You are fully liable for your debt, so I am in no way telling you not to pay, but I am telling you to study and know your rights as a consumer.

# Module 5

## Revolving and Installment accounts

I will help you understand the difference between installment and revolving accounts in this module. Both play a significant role when it comes to your "mixture" of credit and your "debt utilization."

An Installment account has a set payment, fixed interest rate, and term end date (which can be altered if a deferred payment is applied). This allows you, the customer, to properly budget and know what is expected based on your terms and conditions. An installment account can be altered or reconstructed for whatever reason at the customer's request and based on the lender's approval. Interest is accrued and calculated daily based on the remaining principal balance.

A Revolving account has a set limit, variable interest rate, and payment based on the principal balance. A revolving account can be a credit card or a standard line of credit that is a stand-alone account attached to a checking account or a HELOC (Home Equity Line of Credit). Now, this account sometimes comes with an expiration date depending on the terms and conditions. What I mean by this is that a HELOC can be set at $10,000 with a 15-year term, allowing a 5-year period to withdraw the funds. This allows you to have access to withdraw up to $10K for a 5-year draw period, but you are allowed to repay the loan for 15 years.

As a credit card holder, be sure to keep your credit in good health and build rapport with your creditor. This is additive when requesting a credit limit increase and/or negotiating your interest rate. After twelve months of having a credit card, companies will typically review your history with them. Depending on your creditworthiness, they can decrease or increase your credit limit and interest rate. It's not often, if ever that they will decrease your interest rate, they are in business to make money. I encourage you to initiate the call, have a conversation with the creditor, and request an interest reduction.

NEVER close a credit card. Closing a credit card can significantly decrease your credit score. Guess what else it will affect? Never mind; I'll tell you: it will affect your length of credit and available credit. I recommend using the credit card periodically and/or even setting up auto-pay for a reoccurring bill with a small and manageable monthly payment. Some reoccurring accounts may be Amazon Prime, Netflix, Tidal, Hulu, gym membership, etc. Also, do not allow your account to become dormant (no activity/usage) because the credit card company can decrease your limit and sometimes set it to your current balance. Now, you are considered MAXED out on that credit card (ouch). Let's outsmart the credit card companies and beat them at their own game.

# Module 6

## Knowing how to read a credit report

**CREDIT REPORT!**

The fun begins here, but this is honestly the most rewarding tool! Many people won't teach you how to read a credit report. This is 80% of mastering to get your credit score and finances back on track. This diagram will break down line-by-line to identify the terms, codes, and where to look for inaccuracies. This is where many of you have spent hundreds or even thousands of dollars to get your credit repaired because....

1. You just didn't have a clue about what to do.

2. The layout and terms on the credit report seem like a foreign language.

3. It's time-consuming.

4. You have no idea what you are looking at while reviewing your credit report.

The credit report template below will help you with the critical factors to identifying and resolving issues on your credit report that will lead to a better financial situation.

Let's look at your adult report card. Section 609 tells you to look for any inaccuracies that have been reported to the credit bureaus. The first section in your credit report will furnish all your personal information. As you can see below, it provides your name, alias, date of birth, current address, previous address(s), and employer(s).

a. is the actual date you accessed your credit report.

b. Review and identify that your name is spelled correctly and is your name. There are times when a credit report has unknown names to you listed, which could be a red flag. The names you see listed are sometimes an error of the merchant or reflects the information you provided on an application.

c. Make sure that the address reported are accurate and spelled correctly.

d. Remove any old addresses that you aren't associated with anymore.

e. Verify that your employer information is correct.

The information in these sections is imperative when it comes to disputing inaccuracies. As you can see on the Equifax reporting Mr. John's last name is spelled incorrectly. In this case contact the credit bureau and have the inaccurate information corrected. Something else to look out for is when there are family members with the same name and live in the same household. That, too, can sometimes cause inaccurate reporting.

**Personal Information**

Below is your personal information as it appears in your credit file. This information includes your legal name, current and previous addresses, employment information and other details.

| | TransUnion | Experian | Equifax |
|---|---|---|---|
| **Credit Report Date:** | 12/15/2021 | 12/152021 | 12/15/2021 |
| **Name:** | John Uknow | John Lewis Uknow | John L Know |
| **Also Known As:** | - | - | - |
| **Former:** | - | - | - |
| **Date of Birth:** | 7/5/1989 | 7/5/1989 | 1989 |
| **Current Address(es):** | 9876 Southwood Las Vegas, NV 88901 | 9876 Southwood Dr Las Vegas, NV 88901 | 9876 Southwood Dr Las Vegas, NV 88901 |
| **Previous Address(es):** | 12345 Alphabet Lane Los Angeles, CA 90210 | 12345 alphabet Lane Los Angeles, CA 90210 | 12345 Alphabet Ln Los Angeles, CA 90210 |
| | 1522 Swirl Dr Los Angeles, CA 90051 | | |
| **Employers:** | Riverside Medical Center | Riverside Medical Center | Riverside Medical Center |

In the section below, you will identify all reported accounts/tradelines. This section will tell you how many accounts you have in total and the categories they are associated with. You will need to review and verify if there are any reported inaccuracies. Your "Open" and "Closed" accounts should equal your "Total Accounts."

a. In this section, you can see that Equifax only has 2 accounts reported. That means that the creditors either only report to Transunion and Experian.

b. The balances reported should equal the total remaining balances on all accounts, i.e., Capital One's balance is $5000.00, and Best Buy's is $5000.00, so the reported "Balances" should be $10,000.00

c. The section tells you the total monthly payments for all accounts/tradelines on your credit report. In this report, the total payments amount is lower with Equifax because only two accounts are reported when there are, in fact, three open accounts.

d. As stated, inquiries remain on your credit report for 2 years. In this case, Experian has 3 accounts that have not fallen off after 2 years. You can contact Experian and have them removed.

*If there are any "Collection" or "Derogatory" accounts, here's where you will identify what accounts fall into those categories, identify any inaccuracies, and properly dispute those accounts using the correct dispute template.

This section below is a breakdown of your account(s). Each account has its own reporting history, which includes the following: account number, account type and detail, account status, monthly payment, date opened, balance, number of months, high credit, credit limit, past due amount, payment status, last reported, comments, date last active, and date of last payment. This section is where most of your inaccuracies are found. Remember what your rights are and exercise them.

a. Is your account number and should be the correct account number established when you opened the account. It should also match the written agreement you have with the creditor. Sometimes, the account number is missing a number or two, and/or the numbers sometimes do not match on all credit reports, as listed below.

b. This section identifies if this account is a Revolving, Installment, or Mortgage account.

c. This section states the date the account was opened according to your contractual agreement. This can be reporting from your open-end agreement, promissory note, written contract, and oral agreement. If there are any inaccuracies, dispute them. If the account is derogatory and has a negative impact on your "adult report card," exercise your right as a consumer and use the proper "Validation" letter for the account(s).

d. The balance currently owed according to the last reported information from the creditor/furnisher. The payment may be lower or higher in your 'live" account viewing, depending on the payments or transactions made after the billing cycle ended if it's a revolving account and the date of the last payment if it's an installment account.

e. This section is identified if the account is a Mortgage or Installment account.

f.  This is where credit card companies try to make us look bad. The creditors sometimes do what is called a "snapshot" of your account, where they wait until your credit card balance gets as close as possible to the limit and report that to the credit bureaus. This makes it seems as if you are maxed out on your credit card and could potentially decrease your credit score.

g.  Pay close attention to this section to ensure the correct reporting status is represented. On-time and late payments are reported monthly.

h.  This section states what date the creditor has reported/furnished your account history for that month.

i.  Most credit reports will show you a payment history for up to two years for all three credit bureaus. Review this section and identify that all months reported are accurate. Remember, your payment history makes up 35% of your credit score.

The "Bureau" code is what identifies your responsibility with that account. If that section has the letter "I," that means **Individual**, and you are the only person on that account. If there's an "A," that is **Authorized User**, which means someone has added you to their account and gives you the authorization to use their account. This is typically for credit cards. You may also see the code "C" or "J," which means **Co-borrower or Joint**. Meaning you are a responsible party for that account.

CREDITONEBNK

| | TransUnion | Experian | Equifax |
|---|---|---|---|
| Account #: | 987543*** | 987453*** | 9875432** |
| Account Type: | Revolving | Revolving | Revolving |
| Account Type - Detail: | Individual | Individual | Individual |
| Bureau Code: | | | |
| Account Status: | Open | Open | Open |
| Monthly Payment: | $38.00 | $38.00 | $38.00 |
| Date Opened: | 06/01/2018 | 06/01/2016 | 06/15/2016 |
| Balance: | $1235.00 | $1235.00 | $1235.00 |
| No. of Months (terms): | 0 | 0 | 0 |
| High Credit: | | $3615.00 | |
| Credit Limit: | $4000.00 | $4000.00 | $4000.00 |
| Past Due: | $0.00 | $0.00 | $0.00 |
| Payment Status: | Current | Current | Current |
| Last Reported: | 11/30/2021 | 11/30/2021 | 11/28/2021 |
| Comments: | – | – | – |
| Date Last Active: | 11/30/2021 | 11/30/2021 | 11/30/2021 |
| Date of Last Payment: | 11/27/2021 | 11/27/2021 | 11/27/2021 |

Two-Year payment history

Legend

| Month | Feb | Jan | Dec | Nov | Oct | Sep | Aug | Jul | Jun | May | Apr | Mar | Feb | Jan | Dec | Nov | Oct | Sep | Aug | Jul | Jun | May | Apr | Mar |
|---|---|---|---|---|---|---|---|---|---|---|---|---|---|---|---|---|---|---|---|---|---|---|---|---|
| Year | 23 | 23 | 22 | 22 | 22 | 22 | 22 | 22 | 22 | 22 | 22 | 22 | 22 | 22 | 21 | 21 | 21 | 21 | 21 | 21 | 21 | 21 | 21 | 21 |
| TransUnion | | | | | | | | | | | | | | | OK | OK | OK | OK | OK | OK | OK | OK | OK | OK |
| Experian | | | | | | | | | | | | | | | OK | OK | OK | OK | OK | OK | OK | OK | OK | OK |
| Equifax | | | | | | | | | | | | | | | OK | | OK | OK | OK | OK | OK | | | OK |

This section lists all accounts and creditors that have accessed your credit report for any applications you have submitted and/or soft inquiry credit checks are done. Take your time and review this section and verify you have, in fact, applied for any type of credit with these lenders. If there are any unauthorized reported inquiries, contact the credit bureaus to dispute the inaccurate reporting to have them removed.

## Inquiries

Back to Top

Below are the names of people and/or organizations who have obtained a copy of your Credit Report. Inquiries such as these can remain on your credit file for up to two years.

| Creditor Name | Type of Business | Date of inquiry | Credit Bureau |
|---|---|---|---|
| COMENITYCB/BEST BUY | BANK CREDIT CARDS | 12/20/2021 | EXPERIAN |
| NAVY FCU | CREDIT UNIONS | 11/29/2021 | TransUnion |
| CAPITAL ONE | BANK CREDIT CARDS | 09/15/2021 | EQUIFAX |
| CAP ONE | BANK CREDIT CARDS | 09/15/2021 | EXPERIAN |

This section provides contact information for all accounts on your account, whether open or closed. If you conduct disputes directly with the creditors, you will send the proper disputes to the information in this section of your credit report. This is typically the last section on your credit report.

| Creditor Contacts | | ⬆ Back to Top |
| --- | --- | --- |

ⓘ Information about how to contact people and/or organizations that appear on this credit report is listed below.

| Creditor Name | Address | Phone Number |
| --- | --- | --- |
| FACTUAL DATA | PO BOX 530090 ATLANTA, GA 30353 | 800-929-3400 |
| CAPITAL ONE | 15000 CAPITAL ONE RICHMOND, VA 23238 | 800-955-7070 |
| APPLE CARD/GS BANK | P.O. BOX 45400 SALT LAKE CITY, UT 84145 | 877-255-5923 |
| NAVY FCU | PO BOX 3700 MERRIEFIELD, VA 22119 | 803-255-8062 |

As a Certified Accredited Financial Coach, I can't express enough how important it is to handle your credit report and its accounts with integrity. EVERY account/tradeline on your credit report isn't fraudulent account. Remember your rights as a consumer and handle each account that needs attention or has been neglected. Keep in mind that the quick fix is temporary, and those accounts can sometimes reappear on your credit report. The original creditor can also file lawsuits against you which can become more costly.

Have that conversation at the dinner table or in the family/friend group chat, hold yourself accountable, outline your derogatory accounts, review your statute of limitations, highlight the inaccuracies, and send out the proper dispute letter. If it doesn't work the first time, do it again. Take control of your financial peace and freedom. Financial debt can be traumatizing, but your financial peace can be lifesaving.

# Module 7

## The lack of Financial Literacy

As discussed in Module 1, there is a huge lack of education as it relates to financial literacy. Knowing and identifying what credit is, how it works, the gamble of it, budgeting, and savings are now becoming somewhat top of discussion but still not as often as they should be. The lack of financial literacy can become costly. Poor spending habits can lead to the misuse of credit cards, overdrawn bank accounts, and little to no savings. According to CNBC, "A report from the National Financial Educators Council shows that 38% of individuals in a recent survey said their lack of financial literacy cost them at least $500 in 2022, including 15% who said it set them back by $10,000 or more. That's up from about 11% in 2021. The majority (68%) of respondents said poor financial literacy cost them somewhere from zero to $499. The average cost was

$1,819, according to the survey, which was conducted Oct. 23 through Dec. 5 among about 3,000 adults across the country. That 2022 figure is nearly $500 higher than the average $1,389 in 2021."

(https://www.cnbc.com/2023/01/19/heres-how-much-people-say-lack-of-financial-literacy-cost-in-2022.html#:~:text=Investing%20Club-,Lack%20of%20financial%20literacy%20cost%2015%25%20of%20adults%20at%20least,Here's%20how%20the%20rest%20fared&text=The%20share%20of%20people%20who,under%20%24500%2C%20if%20at%20all.)

That is huge when the consumer mentioned that it cost them an average of $10k, calculated based on high-interest rates in credit card usage, longer terms of paying off debt which causes more interest, and a decline in their credit score. A decline in your credit score is sometimes caused by high debt utilization, allowing the creditors to increase your interest rates and lower your limits.

Teach your kids while they are young and allow them to soak up all the knowledge they can. They are a sponge as a child. Make it fun, relatable, and engaging. We are in a time now when we have the advantage of proving statistics wrong.

Here are some financial literacy statistics:

**Key Takeaways**

- 75% of American teens lack confidence in their knowledge of personal finance.

- 25% of Americans say they don't have anyone to ask for trusted financial guidance.

- 23% of US adults ages 18 to 29 have credit card debt that's over 90 days overdue.

- Americans owe over $800 billion in credit card debt as of Q1 2022.

https://www.annuity.org/financial-literacy/financial-literacy-statistics/

The average person does not have $400 in their account for minimal emergency expenses. Your monthly emergency expense account should consist of 3-4x the amount of your monthly bills. To get on track with your savings goals, begin to scale back on unnecessary purchases; you know what they are. It may be hard or sacrificial initially, BUT the ending is so rewarding.

Financial literacy must begin to take precedence in the home and schools to overcome failure and the education barrier of not knowing how to place ourselves in better financial situations. Take the lessons in this book and allow them to become a part of your daily retained knowledge and help others around you.

# Module 8

## The POWER of three numbers

These three numbers seem so small, but they play a huge role in your daily life. Your credit score is not just a set of numbers to identify how you are doing financially. It is basically your adult report card. When I was an underwriter in consumer lending, I would have to make a financial decision for the consumer based on what their credit report said. Was it a biased decision? Absolutely. Your credit report tells the lenders, underwriters, and credit card companies the following: who you are based on your name; address; job; the type of accounts you have/had; how many times your payment was late and on time; the impact of the times you ignored those 1-800 numbers; how long you've had an account open; who's responsible for the debt; and so much more.

It is imperative to take care of and nourish your credit report. Underwriters care nothing about you being an amazing person. They are not impressed that you are wealthy. They are less concerned that you have been a member or customer of their financial institution for 25 years. They are more concerned with how responsible you are and will be with the funds they will lend you. It is unfortunate but true: lenders respect you more and offer you the best products when your credit score is high, debt utilization is low, and you have collateral to back you.

The lower your credit score, the higher your interest rate is. This is where borrowing funds can become costly. Lenders and creditors survive off your interest rate and fees. A low credit score can affect the following: your deposit to move into an apartment or rent a house, your deposit on your utilities if an employer will offer you a job, auto insurance premiums, higher interest rates on auto loans, credit cards, line of credits, and the list goes on.

A loan denial can alter your self-esteem and posture, cause a lack of self-confidence and depression, and alter your daily productivity (it happened to me). DO NOT allow this to overcome the amazing person you are. Life happened, and NOW is your opportunity to take it back. DO NOT allow three numbers to identify who you are. I challenge you to face your financial situation, take the blame but forgive yourself and extend grace to yourself and the person you "co-signed" for (I had to make you laugh). You can do this by following the steps in the "DIY" Module of this book.

# Module 9

## The statute of limitations

The statute of limitations is something that isn't talked about often. This is a law set in place to give creditors a time frame to retrieve funds from an outstanding debt owed by the consumer. Each state has its limitations, and there are 4 types of statute of limitations: via an oral agreement, a written contract, a promissory note, and an open-end account.

- Oral agreement- a verbal agreement between the consumer and lender to pay a debt.

- Written contract- a debt established and agreed upon in writing between the lender and consumer.

- Promissory note - a note signed by the consumer and lender detailing the payment amount, interest rate, start, and end date.

- Open-end account –an account that gives you access to funds just as a revolving account or credit card.

It is imperative to check this often for your state. For example, the state of Connecticut changed its limitations last year from a maximum of seven years to three years, where they can legally seek redemption of monies owed.

If there is a debt owed that is now in collections and or charged off, you will have to identify how long the creditor is allowed to seek repayment of the funds owed. While in the statute of limitations, the creditor can seek legal repayment of funds by way of a lawsuit. You will want to avoid that at all costs. After the statute of limitation has expired, your account is considered time-barred debt. Having debts owed beyond the statute of limitation does not mean your debts are relinquished. They will remain on your credit report and have a remaining negative impact. Yes, the older the debt, the less the weight of the negative impact when it comes to your score. When considering disputing derogatory accounts, review the statute of limitation first and follow your rights as a consumer. In 2021, the state of New York passed a bill called the Consumer Credit Fairness Act of 2021. The bill was enacted and put in place on Apr. 7, 2022. The Act reduced the statute of limitations in New York to three years. Shout out to New York! Below is a chart with the statute of limitations for each state.

# Statute of Limitations

| State | Oral contracts | Written contracts | Promissory notes | Open ended debts |
|---|---|---|---|---|
| | Statute of Limitations as of 2022 (in years) | | | |
| Alabama | 6 | 6 | 6 | 3 |
| Alaska | 6 | 6 | 3 | 3 |
| Arizona | 3 | 6 | 6 | 3 |
| Arkansas | 5 | 5 | 5 | 3 |
| California | 2 | 4 | 4 | 4 |
| Colorado | 6 | 6 | 6 | 3 |
| Connecticut | 3 | 6 | 6 | 3 |
| Delaware | 3 | 3 | 3 | 4 |
| D.C. | 3 | 3 | 3 | 3 |
| Florida | 4 | 5 | 5 | 4 |
| Georgia | 4 | 6 | 6 | 6 |
| Hawaii | 6 | 6 | 6 | 6 |
| Idaho | 4 | 5 | 5 | 4 |
| Illinois | 5 | 10 | 10 | 5 |
| Indiana | 6 | 10 | 10 | 6 |
| Iowa | 5 | 10 | 5 | 5 |
| Kansas | 3 | 6 | 5 | 3 |
| Kentucky | 5 | 15 | 15 | 5 |
| Louisiana | 10 | 10 | 10 | 3 |
| Maine | 6 | 6 | 6 | 6 |
| Maryland | 3 | 3 | 6 | 3 |
| Massachusetts | 6 | 6 | 6 | 6 |
| Michigan | 6 | 6 | 6 | 6 |
| Minnesota | 6 | 6 | 6 | 6 |
| Missouri | 5 | 10 | 10 | 5 |
| Montana | 3 | 8 | 8 | 5 |
| Nebraska | 4 | 5 | 5 | 4 |
| Nevada | 4 | 6 | 3 | 4 |
| New Hampshire | 3 | 3 | 6 | 3 |
| New Jersey | 6 | 6 | 6 | 3 |
| New Mexico | 4 | 6 | 6 | 4 |
| New York | 3 | 3 | 3 | 3 |
| North Carolina | 3 | 3 | 5 | 3 |
| North Dakota | 6 | 6 | 6 | 6 |
| Ohio | 6 | 15 | 15 | 6 |
| Oklahoma | 3 | 5 | 5 | 3 |
| Oregon | 6 | 6 | 6 | 6 |
| Pennsylvania | 4 | 4 | 4 | 4 |
| Rhode Island | 10 | 5 | 6 | 4 |
| South Carolina | 3 | 3 | 3 | 3 |
| South Dakota | 6 | 6 | 6 | 6 |
| Tennessee | 6 | 6 | 6 | 3 |
| Texas | 4 | 4 | 4 | 4 |
| Utah | 4 | 6 | 6 | 4 |
| Vermont | 6 | 6 | 5 | 3 |
| Virginia | 3 | 5 | 6 | 3 |
| Washington | 3 | 6 | 6 | 3 |
| West Virginia | 5 | 10 | 6 | 5 |
| Wisconsin | 6 | 6 | 10 | 6 |
| Wyoming | 8 | 10 | 10 | 8 |

# Module 10

## The Uncomfortable conversation

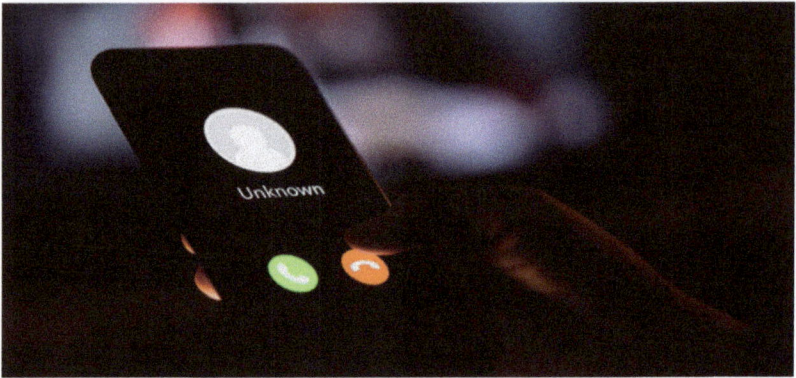

Let's talk about it. What do you do when you see that 1-800 number calling you? I know. Most of the time, you don't answer or send the call to your voicemail (laugh out loud). You must remember that you requested a relationship with that merchant(s). You made a commitment with a PROMISE to pay them back, and they TRUSTED that you would pay them back as agreed upon in your contract. Not answering the phone after multiple attempts will give the creditor ammunition to submit your account to the collection agency. This, in turn, now leads to a bigger problem. Many times, you don't answer because it triggers your financial trauma. It brings stress and anxiety and, in most cases, affects your confidence.

I challenge you to answer the phone and converse with the creditor. Especially before the account is sold to the collection agency and then reported to the credit bureaus. Here are some ways to have that "uncomfortable" conversation:

1. Be proactive and call the creditor once you know there will be a change in your finances.

2. Be vulnerable (tell them the truth and be okay with not being okay).

3. Stress how important your credit is to you.

4. If you decide to settle the debt, ask them for a settlement of 20% of the balance owed. This is the only time I will ask you to go low and let them go high.

5. Ask for a realistic payment arrangement.

6. Once a final agreement has been made, ask the merchant for a written agreement. Never agree based on verbal terms only.

7. Commit to the payment, and if you can't make that payment, call days in advance and communicate your situation to the creditor.

8. Be nice even if they aren't; you can *woosah* after you finish the call. The ball is in their court, and you can't afford to make another foul play.

This now-comfortable conversation will help relieve some of the financial stress you carry. You owe it to yourself. You've worked too hard not to receive the financial freedom that is due to you. Move with integrity and honesty; it will be rewarding in the end.

# Module 11

---

## Who's Who and Knowing your rights!

In the world of financial literacy, there is undoubtedly a lot to learn. In this section, you will learn and make yourself aware of your protections as a consumer. These laws will help you protect your credit, disputing inaccuracies on your credit report and bring awareness of what acts from the creditors are legal and illegal reported. Often, inaccurate reporting remains on your credit report because of the lack of knowledge and understanding. I charge you to exercise your rights. Do not let this section overwhelm you. Take your time and remember, these laws were passed and put in place to protect you. Let's talk about a few of them.

As a consumer, you are protected by "The Consumer Credit Protection Act." This Act was enacted in the late 1960s and comprises several laws protecting your personal credit. It protects it from banning honest credit reports and discrimination. The CCPA (Consumer Credit Protection Act) has an umbrella that consists of five Acts: The Truth in Lending Act, which allows creditors to furnish honest information; The Fair Credit Reporting Act regulates credit reports; The Equal Credit Opportunity Act, which protects you from discrimination when applying for any lending; The Fair Debt Collection Practices Act, which protects you from having debt collectors calling your place of employment, contacting you after certain hours, and harassment; and The Electronic Fund Transfer Act, which protects consumer finances during electronic payments.

CFPB- The Consumer Financial Protection Bureau is a 21st-century agency that implements and enforces Federal consumer financial law. It also ensures that markets for consumer financial products are fair, transparent, and competitive. They are a US government agency dedicated to ensuring you are treated fairly by banks, lenders, and other financial institutions.

( https://www.consumerfinance.gov/ )

FTC- Federal Trade Commission was established in 1914. The FTC was created to prevent unfair methods of competition in commerce. "In 1938, Congress passed a broad prohibition against unfair and deceptive acts or practices. Since then, the Commission has also been directed to administer various consumer protection laws, including the Telemarketing Sales Rule, the Pay-Per-Call Rule, and the Equal Credit Opportunity Act. In 1975, Congress gave the FTC the authority to adopt industry-wide trade regulation rules."

( https://www.ftc.gov/about-ftc )

The CARD Act- The Credit Card Accountability Act was established in 2009. It amends the Truth in Lending Act given to consumers in disclosures, which describes the open-end credit lending procedures, the limits and increased penalties of fees and charges, and constraints and issuance of credit cards to minors and students. It also amends the Electronic Funds Transfer Act, which discusses fees for gift certificates, pre-paid gift cards, and store gift cards. The CARD Act also discloses information about the "Fair Credit Reporting Act by requiring FTC rulemaking to mandate that advertisements for free credit reports disclose that free credit reports are available under Federal law at annualcreditreport.com and by protecting young consumers from prescreened credit offers (Sections 205, 302)."

(https://www.ftc.gov/legal-library/browse/statutes/credit-card-accountability-responsibility-disclosure-act-2009-credit-card-act).

FCRA- The Fair Credit Reporting Act is a federal law passed in 1970. It was set in place to protect consumers as it relates to information that is reported on their credit report. The FCRA helps ensure accurate reporting and the privacy of the consumer. If you are denied a loan, the creditor must provide the reason for the denial following the FCRA law. You are also entitled to one FREE credit report annually.

To obtain your free credit report, visit www.annualcreditreport.com. I encourage you to monitor your credit report monthly and get access to all three credit reports, including your credit score. To ensure accurate credit scoring, you will likely have to pay a monthly fee to a reliable company that will furnish all three credit reports. Most credit card companies now give you access to your credit report and score, which is great, but ensure you have access to all three. Not doing so and trying to restore the health of your credit is like going to the gym every day but maintaining bad eating habits. With that being said, let's work on getting you healthy again.

# Module 12

DIY
# You got this!!

In this module, I will give you a step-by-step guide on taking control of your credit. While working on your credit report, I encourage you to do so with integrity. Reporting ALL accounts as "Fraud" will not help you in the long run. I encourage you to focus on long-term success. As a consumer and according to the FCRA sections 609, 611, and 623, you are entitled to accurate credit reporting. And if it isn't done, you have the right to dispute inaccuracies.

You can send letters to the creditors on your behalf, asking them to identify the reported inaccuracies. By law, the creditor has 30 days to respond to your letter. They are given two options: correct the inaccuracies or remove the account from your credit report if they can not verify your requested information. That is the law!

A law was passed in July of 2022 that any paid medical debts will be removed from your credit report. Also, any unpaid medical debt reporting has now changed from 6 months to 1 year. This means if you have any outstanding medical debt, you now have 1 year to contact your insurance company to ensure the amount owed is accurate, and the correct codes were entered at the time of billing. Starting in 2023, any medical debt under $500.00 will not be reported for collection on your credit report. This doesn't forgive you of the debt; it is still owed. If it becomes a hardship to pay the debt, contact the billing department for that provider and ask them for any "hardship" or grant programs. Work every available option. You have not because you ask not.

Here is a list of letters you can send to the creditors/credit bureaus.

1. Debt Validation letter.

2. Pay and Delete letter.

3. Goodwill letter.

In this section, do not get overwhelmed by this process. Take your time but do not become stagnant while on this journey to financial FREEdom. Let's take a walk....

1. Know and understand your rights as a consumer.

2. Identify what the statute of limitations is for your state.

3. While reviewing each account/tradeline, ensure the reported balance, account number, balance, responsible code, date opened, address, and social security number are correct.

4. Review your credit report and write down what accounts you will need to work on. If it becomes overwhelming, focus on one account per week.

5. Reviewing your credit reports from ALL three credit bureaus (TransUnion, Equifax, Experian) is imperative. Write down the reporting agency for each account. Remember, not every account is reported to all 3 credit bureaus.

6. Identify your credit reporting inaccuracies. Document the inaccuracies next to each account you have identified.

7. Identify which dispute letter you will use for each creditor and mail them signed and certified to the credit bureaus or the original creditor (this will depend on your personal financial circumstances).

8. Allow 30 days for a response.

9. If there is no response in 30 days, send a "2nd Attempt" demand letter. If the letter pertaining to the debt is validated per their research, but you feel there is still some inaccurate reporting, send the letter a 2nd, 3rd time, or 4th time. Their goal is to get you frustrated and give up on putting yourself in a better financial position and exercising your rights as a consumer.

10. DO NOT give up! This process can become overwhelming, but it's ultimately worth it. Nothing like peace of mind. Exchange your time for freedom.

# Credit Bureaus information

**Equifax Information Services, LLC**
PO Box 740256
Atlanta, GA  30374-0256

**Experian**
PO Box 4500
Allen, TX 75013

**TransUnion Consumer Solutions**
PO Box 2000
Chester, PA 19016

# Module 13

## Templates

### Debt Validation

Date:

Name:

Re: Notice of Dispute Pursuant to Section 609(a) of the Federal Fair Credit Act

To Whom It May Concern: (Name of Creditor)

I have recently received inaccurate reporting on my credit report from (Company name). I am disputing the reporting from your company and requesting that (Company name) remove the inaccurate reporting/debt from my credit report. The reporting has caused harm to my credit score and credit health. The information that you reported is inaccurate. This is non-compliant and is in violation of the Fair Credit Reporting Act in section 1681n.

This reporting is unwilful and unjust, and per my rights and protection as a consumer in section 609 of the Fair Credit Reporting Act, you are to validate the following:

- Name of the Account holder

- Account number

- Date the account was opened

- Signed agreement

- Customer address

- Customer phone number

- Original account balance

- Validated current account balance

By law, (Company name) are to investigate and respond to the account referenced within 30 days of this dated letter. Please remove the inaccurate reporting and/or account from my credit report within the time allotted.

Signature

# Pay and Delete

Date:

Original Creditor:

Account number:

The amount owed (from credit report): $

This letter is written in response to the letter received stating the alleged amount of (dollar amount). I/we am writing this letter asking for a one-time request to settle the alleged debt reported above and asking to settle the debt in the amount of (dollar amount). This is in no way agreeing to the debt stated as owed, nor am I acknowledging any liability of the debt. In addition to this settlement request, I ask that the account referenced be removed from the following credit bureaus (insert TransUnion, Equifax, and Experian).

Again, as I disagree with the total amount owed and under the circumstances that the above request is considered and acknowledged in writing, I am willing to settle the amount requested. I am asking that, along with the requested settled amount, (Company Name) remove this account from their database and any collection or third-party companies. And the debt is reported in your records as paid to a $0 balance. Once the settlement is agreed upon, I also request a letter with your company letterhead signed by someone in leadership/management.

Thank you again for your consideration, and I look forward to speaking with someone at your company.

Signature

# Goodwill Adjustment

Date:

Merchant:

Account number:

I have been a customer of your company since (year account started). And I greatly enjoyed my experience with (name of company) during that time. We are writing to see if you would be willing to make a "goodwill" adjustment to your reporting to the three credit agencies. We have (number) late payments on the above-referenced account that date back to (date of late payment(s)). Since then, I have been an exceptional customer paying every month on time and never 30 days late.

With our exceptional payment history over the last year, we would like you to consider removing the negative payments from my credit reports. At the time of the late payments (the reason you missed payment), I say this not to justify why the payments were late but rather to show that the late payments are not a good indicator of my actual creditworthiness. We hope that (name of company) is willing to work with us on erasing these marks from my credit reports.

We have been very happy customers in the past. We hope to continue a long relationship with (name of company). With today's credit industry so competitive, we know how important it is to maintain good customer relationships. (Name of company) has been exceptional in our book so far, and we highly recommend you all to our friends and relatives. We hope you will deeply consider this request and prove again why (name of company) is heads above the rest.

I look forward to your reply.

Thank you in anticipation.

Signature

# Glossary

**Authorized user-** is a person who is given permission by the creditor/account holder to utilize the available funds on their credit card. As an authorized user, you are not responsible for the debt owed on the account. But if there is a missed payment or negative reporting on the account, you will also incur a negative impact on your credit report.

**Closed-end credit-** a financial agreement between the consumer and the lender with the understanding of the set payment, interest rate, and term that dictate for the funds to be repaid.

**Closed Date-** The date the account was closed.

**Charge-Off -** is an account that has become delinquent for a while and is now written off as bad debt for the consumer. The lender has written the debt off as a loss to their company.

**Credit-** the ability of a customer to obtain goods or services before payment, based on the trust that payment will be made in the future.

**Credit** Limit/**Line of Credit-** Is considered an open-end credit account. A line of credit (LOC)/ Credit limit is what the lender has set to be the maximum amount of funds you can access or spend on that account.

**Credit Report -** Is a report that provides information from credit furnishers. It will include new and old accounts. It will contain scoring factors and reporting from all three credit bureaus. You can also now request that certain utility accounts be reported monthly.

**Delinquent -** to be past due on your obligations.

**Debt -** is an obligation of monies owed by the consumer to a lender.

**DTI -** Debt to Income is a calculation that shows the financial worthiness based upon and can be calculated monthly and annually. For your monthly DTI, you must calculate your total monthly payments by your total gross income. For your annual DTI, you must divide your total account balances by your annual gross income.

**Finance charge -** fees that are attached to your loans and credit cards. The charges are added to the last reported balance and are incorporated into your monthly payment each month unless you have an account with a 0% promotion.

**Inaccuracies-** false; not true.

**Interest rates -** the proportion of a loan charged as interest to the borrower, typically expressed as an annual percentage of the loan outstanding.

**Installment account -** is an open account where you have agreed to have a set payment, due date, interest rate, and loan end date.

**Open credit -** a financial agreement between the consumer and the lender with unlimited access.

**Open-end account –** an account that gives you access to funds just as a revolving account or credit card.

**Oral agreement -** a verbal agreement between the consumer and lender to pay a debt.

**Promissory note -** a note signed by the consumer and lender detailing the payment amount, interest rate, start, and end date.

**Revolving account -** an open account where you will have access to funds for an unlimited or set time, and the funds are available to you again as payments are made.

**Time-barred debt -** is debt that has passed the Statute of Limitations and cannot be collected.

**Tradeline -** is an account that appears on your credit report that provides information from the credit reporting agencies. Your tradeline consists of information such as your credit limits, the date the account was opened/closed, the type of account, the name of the company, payment amounts, balance owed, and payment history.

**Written contract -** a debt established and agreed upon in writing between the lender and consumer.

www.ingramcontent.com/pod-product-compliance
Lightning Source LLC
Chambersburg PA
CBHW040910210326
41597CB00029B/5034